BE:
The Humanity Blueprint

INTRODUCTION

An Invitation to BE

IANA LAHI

BE: The Humanity Blueprint Introduction
Published through Spirit Gateways®Publishing

All rights reserved
Copyright © 2019 by Iana Lahi
Cover art copyright © 2019 by Spirit Gateways®/Iana Lahi
Interior Book Design and Layout by
www.integrativeink.com

ISBN: 978-0-9862384-6-8 (Paperback Edition)
ISBN: 978-0-9862384-7-5 (Ebook)

Library of Congress Control Number: 2018910452
No part of this publication may be reproduced, stored in a retrieval system, or transmitted in any form or by any means electronic, mechanical, photocopying, recording, or otherwise, without the written permission of the author or publisher.

To Humanity —

To all women, men, and children of planet Earth

Of all religions, nationalities, and colors

We are One.

Together let us honor life and each other

May the Light within every heart and soul,

Expand. Evolve. Enlighten.™

Into the truth.

Waiting to BE lived.

By You.

BE ONE. BE YOU.™

I have come to sow the seed of love in your hearts so that, in spite of all superficial diversity which your life in illusion must experience and endure, the feeling of oneness through love is brought about amongst all the nations, creeds, sects and castes of the world.
  — Avatar Meher Baba[1]

---

[1] *God Speaks, The Theme of Creation and Its Purpose,* by Meher Baba, Dodd Mead, 1955. Sec. ed. p. 40, 41-55, 155

CONTENTS

Preface 1

Introduction 23

The New Source Codes For Humanity 49

Be Priorities 65

Preface

You and I are ONE. I do not know you, but I do. We are connected through the love in our souls. We share a common thread that unites us. I know that if I were sitting with you right now, you would have something incredible to teach or share with me. I would open to receive who you are and BE WITH YOU. I would experience the BEingness or essence of your Whole Self. This is the energy that people feel from you when you are just being YOU and doing what you came here to BE.

The Real Divine You

You are being invited to experience transforming your consciousness and your life through a new humanity blueprint. It is for adventurers, seekers, creators, lovers, teachers, innovators, explorers, realists, dreamers, leaders, generators, healers, and initiators. It is for the renewal and rebirth of planet Earth, and for our collective enlightenment. *BE: The Humanity Blueprint* provides the universal pathway through the old matrix of global history into a new planetary and personal roadmap of integrated, aligned, and unified Oneness with Infinite Source—a new matrix of living. The mind is ready for a new reality that is aligned to light, wholeness, truth, and abundance. The soul is ready to BE the initiator, generator, and programmer for the body unified in light and freedom. The Spirit is ready to know itself through an awakened consciousness with the Whole Self. The body most of all is crying out to be loved, embraced, and connected to pure light and divine intelligence.

The teachings contained within *BE: The Humanity Blueprint* are offered as a blueprint to who you really are. They are a 21st century practical and divinely-sourced roadmap, with step-by-step instructions to return you to your True Self and your essence as a being of love. The New Source Codes of Humanity contained within these BE books exist to help you remember how to BE Love. BE Whole. BE Integrated. BE Connected. BE One, and simply BE YOU. However, this is not "the you" that you currently know and experience, but the TRUE, REAL, ESSENTIAL YOU that is ONE with INFINITE SOURCE and all life.

The purpose of *BE: The Humanity Blueprint* is to return to each individual the ability to access and integrate the truth, light, power, and love that are an innate birthright. It provides the tools necessary to walk through the gateways of awakening and enlightening into one's True Self. The Spirit gateways are not only for individual freedom but also for the enlightenment of all beings.

BE: The Humanity Blueprint is an integrated process that includes the most integrated teachings and concepts from the pivotal points of humanity's conscious evolution over the last 5,000+ years, with a new paradigm of higher light consciousness that has entered into the DNA of planet Earth. It is *in the body enlightenment*. The deep concepts and truths from many civilizations, enlightened masters, and teachers are re-structured into these teachings for humanity from Ascended Masters, Intergalactic Messengers, Perfect Masters, Hierarchy of Light, and the Avatar of the Age for these times. The teachings and meditations given in BE are direct transmissions from

Infinite Source that I have personally practiced. My motto has been, "Unless personally experienced, I will not share or speak it." They need to work in the now and create an obvious shift in consciousness. Through direct connection with Infinite Source has evolved a structure and framework that unifies the physical-spiritual architecture, science, and engineering of how Spirit and the body work as One.

You will be given the opportunity to reconnect with your Original Self and an original state of BEING that has been missing for thousands of years. You are being given the opportunity to activate your spiritual DNA and light body through clearing, healing, and aligning all of the components of yourself—your physical, energetic, emotional, mental, and spiritual aspects to become whole and ONE.

What makes *BE: The Humanity Blueprint* different is that it is an integrated divine feminine and masculine pathway into the heart of love. The steps given support you to move through the gateways of your heart and soul while BEing deeply connected to Infinite Source. Your soul is made up of both divine masculine and feminine energies, and their union aligns your body, mind, and heart to your higher destiny path.

These teachings are deeply needed at this time. We are facing dramatic light-dark splits in our culture, nations, communities, systems, and hearts. We need new tools to help us move out of lower survival fears into higher survival that is anchored in BEing One with our Whole Self. We each need a blueprint to help us to emerge as the unique expression of love and power that exists within each and every one of us.

As with any opportunity that knocks at your door, you have a choice to make. You can simply choose to read *BE* and then let it collect dust on your bookshelf or in the recesses of your electronic device, or you can actually choose to *live BE*. It is not meant to be a book to help you simply understand truth, enlightenment, or Oneness consciousness. The whole point of this work is to give you a practical roadmap so that your spiritual practice is not something that you "do" separately from daily life, on occasion when things fall apart, or when you are groping for answers. *BE* is about making your spiritual practice "you just you being you" in your daily existence. *You are your spiritual practice.* You are meant to realize, experience, and live Oneness in your everyday life. *BE* reminds you and helps you live it. You are being given the opportunity to live an enlightened life as the truth and Oneness that you are.

Avatar Meher Baba so clearly states this truth when he says,

> *God cannot be explained. He cannot be argued about. He cannot be theorized, nor can He be discussed and understood. God can only be lived....*
>
> *...To understand the infinite, eternal Reality is not the GOAL of individualized beings in the Illusion of Creation, because the Reality can never be understood; it is to be realized by conscious experience. Therefore, the GOAL is to realize the Reality and attain the "I am God" state in human form."*[2]

With every great opportunity, there are not only choices, but also challenges. Even with years of conscious spiritual awakening and practice, I have had many unexpected and sometimes extreme challenges to work through in this lifetime. I have had to trust BEING ME at times when there was nothing to fall back, stand, or rely upon. I discovered after years of going through many life challenges that I felt as though I knew "nothing." Yet this place of nothing allowed me to connect and BE One with everything.

---

[2] Baba, Meher. *God Speaks,* Dublin, CA: Sufism Reoriented, 2010, pg 190.

My spiritual progression was not about me doing things or taking on roles or ways of being in order to get to a higher place of consciousness or enlightenment. I had to face my false Self in order to find my True Self. I had to let go of everything—beliefs, behavior patterns, projections, delusions, and bad relationships—that kept me in illusion and in a state of separation. I had to trust myself and just *BE me* without any agenda, plan, or direction. I couldn't actually do anything except BE. This is when it was brought home to me that enlightening is not about knowing who we are but about how much we can let go and BE the truth of who we are fully expressed in our life. Knowingness doesn't change us, but BEingness will. This is our greatest challenge as human and spiritual beings.

As a light messenger and spiritual wayshower, I had to stop being the person that I was raised to be at a very young age. I chose instead to find and recognize the truth of my being to help navigate through the emotional repression, illness, fear, and pain of my family of origin and within my own Self. I needed to discover the truth hiding beneath every situation that I experienced. At first this was not conscious, but through testing myself, losing myself, abandoning myself, and re-finding myself, I have come to know and be with who I AM.

I was given many life experiences that tested my ability to walk my truth and BE my truth. I made many mistakes and also had many successes. I have held myself back, doubted myself, sabotaged myself, hated myself, and then decided to love myself completely. It all has made me what I am today.

Our ups and our downs, our challenges, heart breaks, sorrows, disabilities, losses, and fears are on our path to help us to find the clear light within us to step out of being less than who we truly are. Life on planet Earth is meant to evolve into greater levels of creation through our human spirit. We each have the capacity to become light bearers and consciously live our life from connection to our Soul.

We each have our own way of facing our life. We often are our own worst critics and enemies, forgetting to love who we are and what we bring to the world. It is my hope that this work can give you the tools you need to walk through your karma and stay true to your dharma (path) with the greatest of strength and clarity. It is meant to help you make the best choices for you and support your direct path to liberation, light, and living love. I have trail blazed a path and followed a road to enlightening with many, many challenges so that your own road might just be a little more direct, clear, and perhaps even easier.

As human and spiritual beings whose purpose on Earth is to embody and BE LOVE, *BE: The Humanity Blueprint* is a long love letter to humanity—to you. It is meant to awaken, enliven, support, and guide you to step into and BE your whole, true, magnificent Self. It is a spiritual resource to peel away the layers of illusion and darkness that have kept you from the truth and reality of life and your union with all that is. It is a more direct, "fast path" to your authentic, original divine love and power.

As you read and practice the spiritual exercises given in all four BE Volumes, be prepared for the abundant spark of divine activation and healing that will take place in between the moments of reading *BE: The Humanity Blueprint*. Whether doing household chores, working out, being in the dream state at night, leading a meeting, being a parent, BEing One with yourself, engaging in a creative activity, or re-envisioning your work, the ignition and connection to your divine wholeness *will* happen.

Whether we as human beings recognize it or not, the world is naturally moving into a paradigm of love. All structures, beliefs, ways of being, and people are being tested and shifted toward a new spiritually integrated consciousness.

The chaos that we see on the outside is a manifestation of the splits that are within ourselves. The old paradigm has created mass fear and illusion through the manipulation and misuse of power and control. Over time, the internal disengagement from our spiritual power on a body and mind level have grown so out of balance that the "external" can no longer fill our internal emptiness. It is time to shift the world by making a huge shift in ourselves. It is time for mastery.

HOW I CAME TO BE

We all come into our lives with a mission and a purpose. Whether our elders and teachers recognize and support what makes us unique or not, our soul consciously or unconsciously does everything that it can to direct and guide us to fulfill our purpose. Along the way, whether through ease or strife, if you choose courage, perseverance, and surrender to higher love, your greater truth will be revealed. The light of your Self has the potential to be revealed at any given moment. There comes a point when your whole life comes together and reveals to you how divinely perfect every experience has been up into the present moment. It provides instantaneous, perfect realization of what you came here to BE.

I was born to immigrant parents in Brooklyn, New York and grew up on Long Island, New York. From a very young age, I lived in an inner world that I now realize was a world where anything was possible. This inner world was filled with light, color, and simplicity, and I could feel, see, and talk to invisible forces. I spent most of my early years alone connected to this special place that no one could see, sense, or understand. I did not speak until the age of four because I was content there.

Looking back, I now realize that I was connected to a higher state of consciousness, which I had no way of expressing.

When I was four, my parents took me for psychological testing to find out what was "wrong." They saw a potential physical or mental disability. I felt perfectly happy inside of myself and could not understand why my lack of speech would be an issue. As an adult, I now realize that I chose not to speak early on because I felt that no one would understand or care about what I had to say. I also had a direct remembrance of my soul on a vibrational level and realized that the bridge into human conversation was challenging for me. I could not find the words to express the reality that I lived within. It was a truly beautiful space of connection and inner alignment. Within my inner world, I felt content inside, but my experience of my outer reality left me feeling like there was still something missing. I came to realize that I had a deep longing for more connection and love.

I wanted to know unconditional love, but even as a small child I somehow "knew" that my family was unable to give it. I quickly learned that "love" was only given if I met certain expectations and did what I was told. I was being raised in a family that only functioned through conditional love. My response to my physical and emotional environment and this version of love was to "split off" from my full light frequency because I felt no space to be myself. I felt as though I did not matter.

The only place that I could turn to find the deeper love that I wanted was God. I wanted to know that God and I were connected and that "It" existed. When I was six years old, I would sit on the floor under the overhead light fixture on the ceiling in my bedroom and talk to God through the light from the lamp. I felt very alone and sad. I would speak to God every night and ask God to make things okay in my world. I would receive enormous comfort from the light. In those precious moments, the ceiling lamp would turn into God. Everything would disappear except the light and the comfort in my heart. I would have glimpses of an expansive zone beyond time and space that felt like home to me. Those were my first moments of remembrance of my True Self and Source connection.

Ironically, in those moments as an uncertain, longing six-year-old sitting on my bedroom floor, the essence of *BE: The Humanity Blueprint* began. I discovered faith in the light. That faith also led me to discover the doorway through suffering and disillusionment. It led me down the road of my life seeking absolute love and peace, both inwardly and outwardly.

I knew from my early years, perhaps before the age of five, that I was seeing and feeling my external reality from a unique place. I had no idea why or how I was experiencing life differently than everyone else in my immediate circle. I yearned to connect and engage from my heart and be connected with love. I had a deep desire to please everyone around me, and when I couldn't do that, I chose instead to follow the promptings and impulses of my soul. I discovered that I could trust the guidance that came from within me. When I listened, I found that I would grow quickly and draw to me the situations that helped me evolve.

When I did not listen, I would create suffering, which I created plenty of to say the least! One thing that I learned on my own spiritual journey is that we are all very human. We make mistakes, we have blockages to overcome, we can still get hurt or sick, and we are always, always learning and growing. In every moment, we all have a choice to make—whether to follow Spirit and the impulses of our soul and highest truth or to remain enmeshed in a world of controls, fears, denial, and illusion. I just chose to break free at an early age, and chose both difficult and self-initiating situations to learn about life and myself through.

I made the choice when I was 14 years old, while reading the writings of Krishnamurti; two years before I had my first experience with the world of meditation through Transcendental Meditation, to discover my True Self. I seem to have been born with the belief system that the world is ONE and meant to be an experience of love and light, not hatred and pain. Through my rose colored glasses, I saw a world where people could love one another. Yet, back then I had no idea how to love or to receive someone else's love. I was confused and caught in between the ambition and light of my soul, wanting to find the voice of my True Self and needing to stay in control to protect myself from the conditional love around me. I created a wall around myself while still trying to discover who I really was.

My TM practice was my first step in helping me find a direct connection to the divine. It catapulted me into studying and practicing many meditation practices to awaken light, energy, bliss, and God within me.

I was surrounded in high school by the intellectually brilliant future yuppies of my generation who protested the Vietnam War. I felt a different surge of passion than my friends. I felt sourced to peace, not violence. I decided in my heart at that time, to help people think, see, feel, and be connected to life in a different way. I felt that positive political and social change could occur through being connected to divine intelligence and then implementing its wisdom into action. Through meditation, I found a connection to life that inspired me to pursue the real meaning of freedom.

At the very vulnerable age of 21, I began having extraordinary experiences with Master Beings of Light and Consciousness who would appear to me from the inner worlds and higher dimensions of Spirit through my meditations, which consisted of opening to universal Source and asking to be guided to remember who I AM. I had many experiences where I could see, hear, and feel their messages and guidance. I would come to know them as the Council of Light.

The Council of Light is a collective of highly evolved beings who embody the multi-dimensional aspects of being human, celestial, ascended, enlightened, and galactic and intergalactic beings. Beings in the Council of Light have come through all of the tests, lessons, and trials in their own individual spiritual paths and have proven their mastery in the realms of universal leadership. Over time, I could identify and hear their names. I chose not to become a channel for their messages but instead to elevate my own frequency to rise up and meet them where they were. I wanted to receive direct guidance to help become a servant of the light and of the divine. Every interaction and everything in my life became a spiritual opportunity for expansion.

I wanted to know what my life would be like if I entrusted my well being to God and followed the training of the Council of Light from within. I wanted to know my soul and how all souls are similar. I yearned to understand why there are so many religions that all have the same God. I sought the path of direct connection to God through the universe and myself. I could feel God somewhere inside, but I felt blocked emotionally. I had no idea as a young adult the extent to which I took on my family of origin's belief systems, pain, and suffering, which had created blocks within me to access my ability to direct my spiritual power.

For much of my life, I watched members of my family sacrifice their greatest hopes and dreams in order to stay and fit into the family lineage expectations. No one in my family of origin did what they wanted to do. They did what they had to do to make a living. My father had wanted to become an engineer, but his father would not allow it. The only choice my father had was to go into the family jewelry manufacturing business. Giving over his will to his father crushed something in him. Being accepted by his father and obeying his father became the path he walked. Obeying my elders was the path I was supposed to walk, too. I was unable to do this. I was destined to find my own path.

I seemed unable to make my life all about making money and excluding my soul. I broke the rules.

I decided that I would have nothing to do with making money like my family. I wanted to live fully and do something I loved, even though I had no direct experience with anyone who made money doing what they loved. I wanted to be true to my soul, and I equated that with following my passion for dance. I decided to dance full time, train, and study with modern dance and ballet teachers in NYC who are now known as the legacies of American dance.

When I was a teenager, Alvin Ailey chose me out of a long audition to be on scholarship with his company, The Alvin Ailey American Dance Theater in Manhattan. I was part of a high school without walls, and it gave me the opportunity to explore and fulfill my ultimate passion. I was one of the few white girls in the Ailey community, and at age 15, I was intimidated. Growing up in lily-white suburbia on Long Island back then was a far cry from feeling at home with girls who knew life from far greater depth of feeling and soul than my German stoic upbringing taught me. I led a relatively protected and superficial life in comparison, and I had learned to build up walls to protect myself from the feelings and experiences that fragmented my heart.

I worked hard to perfect my technique as I tried to connect more deeply with my body. I spent two years at the Boston Conservatory of Music wearing traditional pink tights and black leotards trying to fit into the traditional dance world. I remember the scent of the studios and locker rooms to this day—pungent, old, and depressing. The serious, superficial, and joyless environment and the grey skies of Boston in winter slowly shut down my spirit. I began reading about Isadora Duncan, the American dance pioneer, and yearned to feel freer in my body. I would spend afternoons on the beach choreographing the ways I interpreted the ocean, Spirit, rocks, and sky. Still, I couldn't touch the power or ache of emotion in my soul because I was still holding onto the family pattern of hiding my emotions and soul away. I knew that dance technique without soul was not enough, so it pushed me into seeking the voice and expression of my own soul.

One night, I saw Bella Lewitzsky's dance company from Los Angeles perform, and I saw a choreographic genius that inspired my soul. I read an announcement that Bella was auditioning dancers for California Institute of the Arts, and I spent the next two days straight in audition. I was chosen, and a few months later moved to southern California and began a new life.

When I arrived at Cal Arts, my first memory was coming out to the pool and seeing dozens of naked students lying around the pool sunbathing. This was the early '70s and a time of discovery and going outside of the box. This would be the beginning of exploring living through my artistic muse and finding the essence of what moved me from the inside out.

I was initiated into meditation, bodywork, healing, sex, and the secrets of ballet all in one year. My body began to open up as my soul began remembering who she was. I would block her power and artistic genius for years, but step-by-step I opened. I would see spiritual teachers on the inner planes, and they would speak to me. I would listen. I discovered that when I danced, I would receive not only high levels of spiritual consciousness but also my body learned how to release its tensions and agendas and let go into Spirit until the energy currents would just take me over. I became a channel of energy, a vehicle for light, and I loved every moment of it. I had no idea where it was taking me.

I began creating dance pieces that were transmissions of higher consciousness and light. The dance faculty had no idea what I was doing or what to do with me. I would open up to the essence of my soul and allow time and space to cease to exist. Source energies of light and love would flow through me as I allowed its silent power to create my movements. I would be suspended into a new frequency that would take decades of doing healing work with others and in myself to embody.

My love of dance never ceased, but the universe thrust me into a new world of being trained as a healer. I had never thought about becoming a healer; it just happened. Healers, shamans, mystics, gurus, and poets came into my life to teach me. The first round of beginning to let go of my past had begun.

When the Masters of Light began to teach me, they would appear in my room by walking through the walls and show up when I was meditating. They were all very direct with me in their teachings and conversations. I would have to absorb a lot quickly and learn how to hold their frequency within my energy field to help me translate into practice what they had communicated. I never spoke to anyone about my visitations with these great Master Beings. I would find their pictures in books at spiritual bookstores, and through their guidance I began the initial levels of Spirit and soul training. They had me surrender everything that was important to me mentally and emotionally. I had to learn to let go *in my body* of what I held onto. I had to feel everything. These lessons became the core theme of my path.

They also gave me a powerful spiritual level of support that was very important for my development. During this time, I separated myself from my family of origin to expand and free myself. I had to in order to begin to find myself. I became adept at living in two worlds or more at once and experiencing my soul open. I was having past life recalls and would see my past lives in front of my third eye. I would spend hours a day meditating, listening to the sound current, viewing the light, opening my third eye, then leaving my body and figuring out how to transmit the energies back into my body to transform my consciousness, and then open my heart. I was continually seeing teachers on the inner planes and soaking in all that they shared. My full focus in my twenties was on my spiritual path. I had no idea where I was being led, but I loved the journey.

I was given the great gift of becoming a mother. The birth of my two daughters 18 months apart cracked me open in profound ways. I was able to feel and witness life being created in my body and birthed through my body. My trust in the universe had become strong enough that I could follow my inner spiritual guidance and create two wonderful pregnancies and births. When I was pregnant with my first child at the age of 25, I went for my first pelvic exam with the doctor who was going to be the back-up physician for my mid-wife just in case I needed intervention. She told me that I could not and would not have a natural childbirth because my pelvis was too small. I remember standing there as she spoke, one of the many times in my life that someone would tell me that I would not be able to do something because I was "too much" or "too little," and I put my hands on my hips, looked her in the eyes, and said, "I will deliver my baby through my vagina." I turned around and walked out, determined that I would have the birth experience that I wanted. I chose to not work with her and instead to listen to my own inner guidance and truth.

Months later, I had my first home birth without a midwife present. My midwife was stuck in a snowstorm in Sante Fe, New Mexico without snow tires, and she didn't arrive until 30 minutes after the birth of my alert and bright, blue-eyed daughter. Fortunately, she had taught my partner and I what we needed to do to deliver our baby and deliver the placenta on our own if needed.

When I was pregnant with my second child, I let my new midwife know that I wanted her to come after the delivery just to check on my baby. I wanted to create a holy space with no interference. She was upset about my request but did honor it. I knew that my connection with Spirit and my body were strong enough to guide me, and I had a successful second home birth that lasted two hours. As I walked in a large circle in my living room, I brought in the energies needed to birth my baby. With each contraction, I would stand and breathe and allow the energies to move through me and open me further. My baby was born as I was standing in a ballet "2nd position."

I discovered that if I practiced inwardly dancing and moving currents of light through my spine and inside my body, that I could increase my sensitivity to the baby's positioning inside of my uterus. Delivering both my children at home was the beginning of living a new lifestyle where everything I chose to think, feel, eat, act upon, and "BE with" shifted and changed me. I was dedicated to helping my children stay connected to their spiritual and creative energies and chose to home school them. This became my greatest joy. Raising my children and seeing them as my inspirational teachers taught me how to love unconditionally, become whole, and take responsibility for my own thoughts and actions. They helped me to rediscover the innocence and beauty of the human Spirit.

In the years that followed, I furthered my training as a healer directly with Spirit. For decades I was put through many disciplines, hardships, and tests. I had to learn to see a situation and a person not from my mind but from the inner eyes of my soul. Instead of just focusing in my heart center, I realized that I had to learn how to integrate light and its power in my lower belly, heart center, and third eye simultaneously to BE connected to the power of my Whole Self. This took me many years to master. When I felt aligned and integrated, I could see and recognize the core issues that I was being asked by my God Self to face. My requests to the universe were to show me how to heal the separations that prevented living in a state of wholeness and Oneness with God—Infinite Source. These requests were answered, but it took me years of learning how to integrate the soul, energetic, emotional, psychological, spiritual-physical insights, and practices that were being given.

As time went on, I learned how to integrate the energies of my higher consciousness through what I would call the "*Power Point Centers*" in my body to increase my connection to the light. These expanded chakra points, when aligned with soul level shifts, catapulted both my Self and my clients to make rapid shifts. My clients were able to quickly move through the karmic and ancestral patterns that blocked them from stepping into their life work with amazing success.

Total awakening involves seeing the light and dark within our energy and Bodymind matrix that block us from BEing in our True Self and to understand how these forces work in the universe. I had to learn to see dark and unawakened energies in their stuck and controlling forms, and through co-working with the Council of Light, I went through many learning curves that humbled, exhausted, and enlightened me. Sometimes I had to help free a person's soul or a collective group of souls, remove a mental or physical illness from a persons "energetic grid," clear an earth portal from Atlantean times, open a city of light above a major metropolitan center, or other intergalactic work.

My physical body went through many challenges to be able to handle the demands of freeing energies to be liberated from darkness into light. This is one of the reasons that I began to eat as consciously as I could. The foods that I ate became balancers for my body and helped me to become a conduit for light energy. I found that if I ate organic vegetables and fruits with compatible proteins for my body chemistry that I could maintain my equilibrium for being a pure channel for the divine. I could build mental and physical stamina and strength as I worked with light and dark energies. I had to learn to BE fully integrated with life force and the higher truths of God—Infinite Source—to develop my skills.

The gift of being able to work with the light and dark and liberate people has been remarkable, but it also has had a spiritual and physical cost. At the beginning, I experienced extreme projections from individuals who had not yet stepped into their spiritual-physical divine wholeness. I went through a time when the more I stepped into my light and power, the more I was judged, rejected, and betrayed. The more light and power I brought forth, the more darkness and fragmentation came out in individuals around me. I realized my light and wholeness triggered people. They would unconsciously want what I embody and get angry because they couldn't feel or access it in themselves. I also realized that their judgment reflected my own self-judgment and self-betrayal. The more inner work that I did to heal the splits in my own mind, heart, and psyche, the more harmonious and healed my energy field became. I took greater responsibility to end the cycles of self-judgment and the subtle judgment of others. My fear and role in creating "my side" of these life challenges could begin to heal and stop the projections.

I was still carrying a lot of self-doubt and feelings of not being good enough. I had more layers to strip away. I also had to learn how to build strong shields to protect and take care of my core Self. I eventually stepped into being and living in the center of love within myself, and this shifted everything for me and for everyone else who came into my life.

I moved through these challenges by building my inner spiritual strength through deepening my relationship and reliance to my heart. I maintained a practice of BEing One in my third eye, whole body, heart, and soul to receive inner guidance. This wasn't always easy and tested my commitment to being a vessel of love and power. Our highest and greatest work is to re-find, rediscover, and reconnect with our true divinity and connection to Infinite Source within our heart and BE IT.

PREFACE

Since being a little girl, I have wanted to BE ONE with Infinite Source. Through many joys and sorrows, I've learned that it is up to me to either become ONE with the wisdom and power of Infinite Source or to live from fear and denial. To stay in fear and denial would mean I would continue to repeat the cycles of suffering and pain that I unconsciously believed were real. As an adult, I would draw the people into my life who would ultimately prove to me that my core belief about my Self was true. I questioned whether I really did have a right to exist BEing me. It certainly is true that we often must get tired of the same old patterns repeating over and over again before we finally are able to make a permanent change. The desire to know how to live, BE, and love from the depths and heart of my soul has consistently moved me forward on my path.

I had to acknowledge my own existence in this lifetime. There was no one in my family of origin who "played the role" in my life script to believe in me. At the tender age of eight, my mother would violently slap my face as she would yell, "You are never to speak your own thoughts like these again, do you understand?" As tears rolled down my cheeks, I struggled with reality and whether to hide away my feelings or to speak them no matter what. My thoughts and words were of my soul attempting to express a perspective of light, insight, and wholeness that challenged my mother's comfort zones of control and self-absorption with her ego, which she chose to live in for the rest of her life. Our experience together helped me to embrace pain with unconditional love. In time, I realized the ultimate gift she had given me—to trust the light of God within my heart and soul, speak its truth, and to BE its presence. This awakening would empower me to help others come through their life obstacles, no matter how heart shattering, and to make the connection with their own inner truth and light blazing from within their heart.

As I received more training and guidance from the Masters of Light, my true voice, self-esteem, and self-worth issues emerged to be dealt with. I realized after decades of training that I would have to accept who I AM first before anyone else could. The more the Masters gave, the more my heart opened, and I had to face how afraid I really was of the light and its power within myself. It is so true that as human beings we don't fear our failure and inadequacy as much as our true light, power, and magnificence. Most of us choose to hold onto the obstacles and controls that we create that prevent us from becoming whole, vital, light-filled, and clear. I was quite adept at creating behaviors that prevented me from stepping into my full light and power. Still, I wanted to BE my full light so much that I was willing to face my greatest fears and pain.

I recognized early on that I was not only carrying pain from this lifetime but also from previous lifetimes where I experienced abuse, abandonment, persecution, control, betrayal, and violent deaths. The enormous pain in my inner feminine energies came from more than the abuse and emotional abandonment from my mother as a child and young adult and from being in a disempowering and controlling marriage. I had chosen those situations because of the inner beliefs I held for myself.

I discovered that I had been a wayshower of light for lifetimes and began to unravel and bring together the golden treasures from my past lifetimes so I could heal the core themes of my soul in this lifetime. I eventually moved beyond my suffering and found freedom through breaking through the inner battles and traps of duality within me that were the cause of my pain. When I talk about pain, I talk about the deep ache, experienced as suffering and longing, to know who I am, what am I here for, what am I really about, why I feel so alone, how can I breakthrough, why can't I step through all the way into BEing fully realized? Pain so many have felt and still do.

The outer and inner transformations experiences that I have come through taught me about the spiritual death and rebirth process. As I continued to let go of the old ways, beliefs, and wounds that held me back, I was being reborn into the light of my full Self, one step at a time. My breakthroughs required that I learn how Spirit works on all planes of consciousness. I came to see that there is a reason for everything that happens in life. Human beings and life itself are multi-faceted and multi-dimensional. Most of us are just not awake to it. As I experienced hundreds of spiritual deaths and rebirths, my inner connection with Infinite Source was the only stabilizing force that could guide and stabilize me. I chose to feel, see, and BE from my heart and discovered that I could move through my life experiences with greater awareness and growth by keeping my heart open. Through feeling and seeing through my heart, I learned how to BE with life—the good and the ugly, wisdom and ignorance, struggle and release, power and disempowerment, and eventually BE One with them all, and to just BE. Learning fearlessness became my path.

There came a point where I knew the pain I had come through was the same pain that all people experience. We share in this pain together whether we know it or not. We are all connected, and what one person feels and experiences, we all experience. As humanity moves through the illusion of separation and outgrows the need to create suffering for others, we will be able to live on planet Earth as God originally intended.

I have consciously chosen to live outside the box of conventional reality most of my adult life—first, as a way to find myself and to BE authentic and secondly, as a way to develop my relationship with the beauty of nature, my spiritual gifts, my inner teachers and Infinite Source as a lifestyle. I have faced physical death more than once and have known chronic illness with an intensity that has taken me into the inner mysteries of my own being. I have lost outer love and found the love within myself. I have embraced challenge as a doorway into higher consciousness. I have faced my deepest wounds. I have learned how to live in the center point where Spirit and the body meet. I have faced coming into Oneness and leaving it, and then having to re-find my way back in. Only when I could release everything with which I had identified myself, could I really reconnect with the truth of my soul and being. I had to learn to let go completely until there was no more self-identifying "I."

Life has taught me that we are here to BE fully expressed as the essence of our heart and soul and make a difference in the world by how we treat one another and care for one another. From this perspective, our new financial, social, educational, familial, political, and business systems can and will evolve.

I am not a spiritual leader or teacher who is above life, sanitized, and in a "neat and tidy" package. That would be an illusion, and I'm all about breaking through the illusion and insanity that we have all called "normal life." My life process of awakening to how God—Infinite Source—lives in me as me, "my Self," has opened healing gifts that were startling even to me. Fulfilling my destiny path meant honoring my own gifts through assisting others to step into fulfilling their highest potential while BEing of service to humanity in a healthy, whole, and integrated way.

Know that I am simply a messenger and an embodied example of the Oneness that is already within you. I am here to guide you to activate the light within you and to BE the full expression of your light. I am your guide to support you to step through what hurts the most, what you fear the most, and what has the potential to take you off of your soul path and help deliver you into BEing your full potential. I will help you find, see, and walk through the gateways into your Self where you will find everything that you have ever wanted and perhaps did not even know existed. After you walk through your own illusions and embrace who you really are, there is nothing left but to BE.

Introduction

*W*elcome to *BE: The Humanity Blueprint.*

All of life lives within you. The five elements; the polarity of the sun and the moon; the movement of the solar system; the essence of all animals, goddesses, and gods; the vibration of stones; forces of nature; the strength of Spirit; and the essence of your soul all make up who you are. What an incredible being you are! What incredible beings we all are! The golden thread that weaves all of us together is the love from Infinite Source.

Imagine being given a roadmap from Infinite Source that helps you to discover the unique qualities, gifts, purpose, and abilities that live within you. Its mile markers include unknown empowerment and unexpected love. If you discovered there is a way to awaken your human and divine energies to take the next steps of your life with greater clarity, power, confidence, connectedness, and trust in yourself and the universe, would you do it? If you knew there was a doorway or a gateway to complete wholeness and connection and someone gave you the key, would you take it? The roadmap, gateway, and key exist within you. They are already yours encoded within you.

The path of your life has been full of twists and turns, and hills and valleys. As human beings living our everyday existence, we experience the highs and lows of our emotions, thoughts, and physical well-being. We often struggle with our thoughts and beliefs, become stuck or fearful, lose ourselves, wonder how to step into passionate and joyous living, get side-tracked by our ego, and so much more. Amidst all of this, within each and every one of us there exists the inner capacity to become ONE, whole, complete, and connected with the infinite and divine intelligence of the universe that exists within us.

There are connections in you, right now, that have gone unnoticed and untapped. Once ignited, they serve to help you become ONE with infinite and divine intelligence. They are *your source and light*, and they are tied with Infinite Source and the light of the universe. When activated, aligned, and expanded, you have a direct line of communication with the universe to help you experience BEing One with the light, joy, peace, and the love within you. The things in our lives that are most meaningful become sustainable. Health, love, exuberant creativity, living on purpose, fulfilling our mission, making money doing what we love, being in loving and fulfilling relationships, and integrating the expansion of the Self become an everyday lifestyle.

BE: The Humanity Blueprint is a gift from Infinite Source to humanity. It is a set of instructions on spiritual integration and ONENESS. Most fundamentally, it is about how to just live and BE in life and BE YOU in a completely whole, integrated, and connected way.

What is happening on the planet?

The world is changing in ways you can see and feel, and in many ways you may not yet know. All of us who inhabit the Earth at this time are alive at a momentous point in human history. We are bearing witness to an energetic shift in the consciousness of all beings on this planet. We are being given a window of opportunity to evolve into a new matrix of consciousness and love that will fundamentally transform what it means to be human and alive. We are being gifted with a new way to access the truth within our souls, rediscover the existence of our divine masculine and feminine energies, and open to a dimension of light and love that once stepped into has the ability to completely shift how we function in our everyday lives.

From the beginning of time, there have been Source Codes to assist humanity live in alignment with Infinite Source. The Source Codes given in *BE* teach how to live in conscious union with the Infinite Source, offering everyone the tools to experience direct connection with a state of consciousness that in the past only mystics, seers, prophets, and perfect masters would know. The New Source Codes of Humanity activate the light to unify, heal, and align the body, mind, and soul to experience greater alignment and reconnection to the Source of our infinite and spiritual intelligence so that we can direct our lives from BEing Whole.

Humanity has come a long way through its battles—sometimes humbled and sometimes not, but always united through its determination to survive. The innate wisdom of humanity and its desire to evolve and grow closer to its original rhythm, pulse, and presence with Infinite Source lives within the cells of every living being. Our hearts and souls have always been ONE with Infinite Source. The pain on a cellular level created by leaving and separating from our original divine connection has taken all of us on a wild and incredulous "ride" through the universe. We are coming closer to realizing that we have the choice to live in separation or to think, feel, and BE in Oneness.

Collectively it is time to "up level" our energetic and cellular energies, which will raise us into a higher frequency zone. This zone holds the codes to creating solutions to the devastation that is occurring on our planet through careless greed, control, and lack of responsibility for ending suffering. The only way to heal and transform the pain that we have perpetuated and continue to create and endure is by our efforts to individually and globally enlighten together. Our humanness needs to be seen and received by other like beings who are also awakening. To come back into our core, we must release and clear the false projections placed upon us over thousands of years emotionally, spiritually, and mentally, and reconnect our soul, heart, and Spirit back together again. Together, we can take the next steps of humanity's awakening and live as the divine BEings that we are meant to BE with greater ease and grace.

To get there, it requires taking a road less travelled. It begins with your own willingness to grow. Only through the awakening and realization of our souls, and their divine feminine and masculine energies within each of us, can we and the Earth survive the cosmic, spiritual, physical, and psychic shifts we must face. Only through a realignment and union of our essential love and power can we rediscover the crucial direct connection with Infinite Source that has been missing for several thousand years. We don't have much time. New skills are required to navigate within this new planetary alignment and paradigm. BE will give you what you need.

A new power and definition of love are being ignited—
They resonate and resound in truth
And have the power to strengthen, heal, and reunite us.

Illusion exists all around us, and as a collective we are bombarded with imbalanced, disconnected, and ungrounded ways of thinking and living. We witness the misuse of power, ethics, and ego consciousness from all sides. We, humanity, need tools that teach us how to become and stay aligned with Infinite Source to break through the illusions of 21st century living. To

INTRODUCTION

face the grand illusions of our time, the first impulse might be to ask, "What can we do to change?" The truth is *there is nothing to change—only illusions, fears, and projections to release.*

During these times, it is essential that we learn how to let go and release what we each believe and hold on to be "true." We must learn to release the beliefs, behaviors, and habits that have served as chains keeping us from the greater truth within our souls. We have new decisions to make and more extensive dreams to fulfill that go beyond the old dreams of simply buying a house, raising a family, and owning two cars. It is time to rebirth some very old abilities, long forgotten. It is time to birth new inner capacities that are yet-to-be expressed and implemented on the planet. It is time to remember what makes us strong and aligns us to living our deepest truths.

We are being called to clear our past and rebuild a lost energy grid that is within our bodies so that we can advance and evolve in love instead of through hatred, fear, ego, and pride. In every moment of our lives, we are being asked to love ourselves and embody love with absolute commitment.

The old ways of how our culture and society have taught us to live and survive just do not work anymore. We have been taught to lose our essential Self, live in mental compartments, and in fear, projection, control, and denial. We are attached to winning, being more self-centered than centered in Self, judging each other and ourselves, and excessively wanting more. We have been taught that who we are is not enough and unworthy of having a voice. We separate ourselves from love as a way to survive and have created personal and global suffering, lack, pain, and sadness through reenacting our "stories," which support our belief system about ourselves.

The new cycle that we face has *never happened quite like this ever.* We are walking forward together into new territory. The new terrain we are entering involves unleashing a new love and power that is found within the truth of our hearts and living in alignment with the power of our soul. By integrating the spiritual currents of light in the brain, limbic and nervous system, energy and auric field, heart center, mind, and soul, we can step into the new paradigm of manifesting our visions, dreams, life purpose, and higher destiny path through love. Living in the head and excluding the power and truth within our body, soul, and Spirit does not work. It once worked as a model for controlling the masses. But now, it is time to place humanity first.

BE: The Humanity Blueprint teaches the steps to live and prosper in the new paradigm of BEing as an integrated human being.

Living on planet Earth in a conscious way requires a new set of skills. To live in alignment and integrity with what is *real* demands being able to access and put into action the whole YOU. Beyond everyday habitual thinking exists an energetic impulse of life force energy that has the ability to guide us beyond our attachments to living in illusion and fear. As light travels from the heart of the universe, it ignites and expands the impulse of living fully connected and unified. The impulse of your life force originates in Infinite Source and is experienced through the vibration of your soul—which is the power and love found in the divine, the essence in your heart and the seed consciousness of your Original BEing.

Millions of people are feeling this spiritual evolutionary impulse. They hear the call to BE, love, and live their lives in a new way. Not everyone takes the call, but many are. They say YES to the truth and possibility of life and who they really are. Will you? If you have already said yes, are you willing to go further? In this work, you will be shown the steps forward on this spiritual adventure. You will learn how to trust what you discover and how to permanently be inspired and ignited to live interconnected to all aspects of you. The days of emotionally and psychologically evolving without the inclusion of a whole soul-body-mind integration can no longer work. Who you are and how you show you up in the world really matters.

Here you are. Here stands all of humanity with the opportunity to live life from a new internal point of integration. It is a place within where love and power, light and dark, and masculine and feminine merge to awaken a light so bright that when allowed to BE, it will enlighten us to our greatest heights of BEing. This is the next evolutionary phase on planet Earth.

Where does this work come from?

In 1976, in Sedona, Arizona, I began a cycle of my life that continues to this day. I was given the message and instruction through a series of synchronistic events that I would be trained in the ways of Spirit, both traditional and from the future. My life has been and continues to be in service to mastering and giving these teachings.

The work that I was given to do in this lifetime is to bring conscious awareness of BEing One with the Whole Self through divine masculine and feminine union and integration. Through activating and integrating the body, mind, and soul into a new paradigm of light, the realization of the True Self through love and Oneness can occur.

I set out on a mission over 40 years ago to discover the common language of the soul that extends beyond nationality, religion, race, creed, gender, or other forms of identification. I discovered that men and women experience and store their emotional wounds in their bodies in different ways, but they have the same needs in their soul. Men and women process feeling and thinking in completely different ways. Both have experienced being shamed, repressed, hurt, and victimized in dissimilar and similar ways, which leads to the fragmentation of our souls and the desire to find union with the divine either directly or indirectly. When I discovered how deeply wounded the masculine and feminine aspects of our self are, and how their separation has created the pain underlying all health issues, psychological problems, relationship issues, and addictions and were the root of the political, educational, and financial breakdowns that the world was going through, and the root cause of sexual abuse and its misuse in relationships, I realized that to move out of the old paradigm and splits of consciousness that we have endured for so long, that we each must find our *divine masculine and feminine soul aspects* and heal our Original Split. As a human race, we have no choice but to come out of denial. We no longer have the option of playing out the scenarios of falsehood and the delusions of the ego. The process of unraveling and coming through stored layers of false beliefs, stories, and ancestral, karmic, familial, and genetic energetic patterns as directly as possible, without emotional drama, became the focus of my work.

How to crack the codes of our ego, fear, pride, and arrogance with love and grace, so we can manifest our life through BEing who we really are, came together through years of discovery and application of the spiritual tools and experiences that I received.

The light teachings and practices shared in *BE: The Humanity Blueprint* are the Original Way Teachings, embodied by Issa (also known as Jesus or Yeshua), St. John the Baptist, St. Francis, Guru Nanak, Shimiz Tabrizi, Hafiz, Kabir, Lalla, Shirdi Sai Baba, Avatar Meher Baba, Anandamayi Ma, Trayambak Nath (Mahavatar Babaji), Melchizedek, Metatron, the Arcturians, El Morya, Sant Kumara, Serapis Bey, Kuthumi, Paramhansa Yogananda, Ramana Maharshi, Divine Mother in her forms of Meryemana (Mother Mary), Mary Magdalene, Kali Ma, Durga,

INTRODUCTION

Tara, Kuan Yin, and many other great beings holding the torch of divine truth.

Throughout the years of my spiritual training, direct knowledge was spoken and taught to me by these Masters of Light and eventually by the Avatar of this age. Each gift of information they shared with me, or transformational experience, was delivered "in person" as a direct transmission, sometimes over several months or years. I would enter the spiritual realm through my heart, soul, and Spirit and my master teacher would shimmer in the physical world in front of me and be seen through my third eye. Together we would meet in the center, where the physical and spiritual realms interconnect. I would take notes, practice what they said, laugh, cry, and look forward to putting it into practice. They had me integrate what I was taught and then immediately apply it with my clients, who experienced radical shifts and results that catapulted them into living their life from their Whole Self while being healed in mind, body, and soul. I realized the miraculous results of my clients were from what I would eventually call the Original Way.

The Original Way Teachings embrace love, living beyond duality, letting go, and releasing your ego identity, discovering your True Self and living in a place of union within your integrated Self—your Bodymind and soul. They reveal the sacred geometry of your higher Self and how the essence of God is coded in your Self. They reveal and awaken your spiritual DNA to transform who you are as a being of light while living in this world—BEing all that you came here to BE.

The Original Way Teachings were once the revered trainings that social, spiritual, and political leaders would begin as children. These teachings remain in our DNA as integrity, justice, the pursuit of truth and freedom, and love as a code of ethics. Throughout history there have been women and men who have chosen to live in alignment with Infinite Source and BE their

Whole Self, with the intention of guiding humanity beyond their fears, pitfalls, and limitations into the next phase of conscious co-creation and evolution.

Perfect Masters, Avatars, Prophets, Mystics, and Divine Messengers have always brought Source Codes to humanity. Source Codes are the activations needed for a specific time period to evolve the consciousness of humanity upward. For hundreds of years, human beings have built upon and implemented the codes from the past. Yet today, humanity no longer has the needed mind and body connections to embody the higher truths delivered by our past spiritual wayshowers.

In the New Source Codes given in the BE books and trainings, the light and dark within humanity are transformed into Oneness. You are guided to experience the alignment needed to maintain your unique mind, body, and soul integration, so you can creatively open to the enlightened field of consciousness within you. These DNA activations give you access to BEing in the total integration of your human and Divine Self.

We are at a critical mass of holy shifting in consciousness—awakening and igniting—at a quantum DNA level. These codes create the awakenings that take you full circle from *a state of evolution into involution.* This is not a state of negative contraction but the inner path of the human soul awakening to its True Self. Avatar Meher Baba speaks of involution as the inner journey of the individual back to its origin through higher planes of consciousness.[3] As the Avatar of this age, Meher Baba created the inner spiritual structure for a new humanity to be birthed through the soul being awakened to its direct relationship to God.

These breakthroughs happen through walking through the gateways of light within your body rather than having to become something or believe in something to evolve forward. By

---

[3] *God Speaks, The Theme of Creation and Its Purpose,* by Meher Baba, Dodd Mead, 1955. Sec. ed. p. 40, 41-55, 155

INTRODUCTION

magnetizing your body-mind-soul with the light and power of Infinite Source, you are able to experience yourself as your true presence and infinite potential.

The BE work is the journey of aligning your frequencies and consciousness into the light of who you are—your God Self. As your sanskaras (projections and illusions) and layers of energetic patterns within you are balanced, the veil over your consciousness and very BEing is lifted, enabling you to rise into your Original Self through your heart—while BEing One in your body, mind, and soul.

What is *BE: The Humanity Blueprint?*

BE: The Humanity Blueprint is a 4-volume roadmap that takes you through the eye of the needle of your consciousness. The exercises, meditations, tools, and guidance in volumes I-IV were downloaded through Spirit to me over many decades. Memories of what I once taught and practiced as a spiritual teacher in past lifetimes came back to me as I dove deeper into my Self and have been the inspiration for the work. My commitment to my own inner work and healing has helped me to bring this work to you. All of the wisdom and practices awakened within me from the universe and my higher Self have helped my clients and students clear, heal, align, integrate, and implement their greatest strengths and truth.

BE: The Humanity Blueprint empowers you to harness your spiritual truth and power and to live your every day life in trust that you really are One with Infinite Source. You are guided into a zone of awakened presence where you are thinking, feeling, and BEing from your whole and multi-dimensional Self.

In *BE* you are given the tools to enter into the abundant, truthful, powerful, and loving inner creation that is your gift from the universe. You are given the way to move through all of the levels of conscious co-creation with your Whole Self and then onward into a new partnership with Infinite Source. Along the way, you will experience what is true for you and find the inner connections to live the life that you are meant to live.

The purpose of the BE work is to guide and support you as a lighthouse of change, love, and brilliance in your life work, career, relationships, community, and in the world. As the inner walls tumble down within you that have blocked BEing who you really are on a soul level, a new rebirth into your Whole Self can occur.

Whether you have an immense connection to Infinite Source, something in the middle, or none, the tools in *BE* will set you free and help you love, BE, and put into action your most soulful and Spirit-driven desires. The world needs you now in your Whole and complete state more than ever. *BE* wants you to BE financially, creatively, spiritually, and infinitely expressed. As you free yourself, the gateways into higher light are opened and will ignite the collective consciousness. You must remember that you are a major player in the evolution of this planet and deeply needed for the world to progress into its highest light for the benefit of all.

As you read *BE* Volumes I-IV, keep in mind that all of these processes weave together simultaneously. The spiritual journey is a spiral process, not a linear one. There is no direct "straight" line to self-realization. Each volume is written to guide you on this adventure in a non-traditional, step-by-step manner. You are being guided to walk through the portals of your own freedom, breakthroughs, and Oneness with Infinite Source. As you follow the guidance in *BE* and progress through your soul, emotional, physical, and energetic realities, you will begin to feel yourself living in many dimensions at the same time. You

INTRODUCTION

will not be looking at your life linearly. Instead, you will feel yourself becoming ONE with the circle of life—your life.

Know that as your soul energies open, you will begin to feel a new movement of energy in your life. Remember that this wave of evolution is happening in everyone's life right now whether they choose to consciously work with it or not. Your soul "just knows" that there is a new experience to be had during these times, and as you progress along through *BE,* you will find a new level of inner trust and security that stabilizes you and gifts you with "grounded and enlightening" confidence and courage.

This journey is not taken from the mind but rather through the soul. It is not about understanding consciousness and Oneness, but experiencing and realizing it. If there is something that you do not understand, read it from your heart. Stop and breathe. Ask Infinite Source to help you receive the seeds. Open to go beyond how your mind creates resistance. Give gratitude for your life. If you follow this roadmap, you will fulfill the path of union with the divine from your heart. Not your head. A new way of being, receiving, and perceiving will open for you. I promise.

The *BE* book volumes will take you on your journey back to your True Self through providing clear, concrete steps and practices that can be implemented to meet your needs and desires.

In Volume I: *One In Soul,* you will be guided through reconnecting the facets of your soul that contain your spiritual light and power. You will discover how to integrate the voice, power, love, and truth that are waiting within you to be found. The clearing, reconnection, and alignment of your soul aspects will elevate you on the "right track" to fulfill your life's calling and destiny.

In Volume II, *Whole Body Enlightening,* you will be guided to heal the energies and beliefs that block your ability to access the light, power, truth, love, and core spiritual experience of being in your body. You will learn about your core wounds and how they heal by opening into your heart center, transforming your psyche, and outgrowing and releasing your layered ego. You will better understand the journey of your own healing into wholeness through integrating your mind and body into your spiritual light and grounded power. You will be prepared for the profound breakthrough work in Volume III and IV.

In Volume III, *Divine Masculine and Feminine Integration*, you will meet the essential and life-changing energies of your inner divine masculine and feminine and their purpose that are unique to you. They open the door to reveal your True Self and give you access to the gateways into Infinite Source. You will learn to listen, feel, and experience the life guidance that your divine masculine and feminine energies want to bring to you. Their wisdom, direct instructions, and divine love and power will shift you into perfect alignment with your life path and clear the way for enlightening your life and living your life purpose.

In Volume IV, *The Union of Infinite Love and Power*, you will be guided through the understanding of how light and dark work and into the self-discovery of how the integration of love and power aligns your life into Infinite Source to accomplish your life goals and desires. You will learn a new perspective about sexuality and your Divine Self and how to navigate your evolutionary pathway. This work helps you fulfill your universal and personal mission, and live in relationship to the multi-dimensional aspects of your whole BEing based upon the Source Codes of Humanity.

BE: The Humanity Blueprint teaches you how to integrate core facets of your soul that make you unique and distinctively you. You are shown how to reunite your body and mind, your higher Self, awaken and heal your heart, break through ancestral and karmic codes, release the debilitating relationship with your ego, transcend fear, discover the power of your soul hiding within the dark places of your psyche, transform into the light of your True Self, know yourself as a spiritual and divinely human being in every moment, turn your past and present lifetime lessons into the knowledge that will set you on your highest destiny path of accomplishment and service in this lifetime, and much more. You will experience feeling ONE with your Self, your life mission, and the universe. You will understand how your lower survival beliefs can be shifted into higher survival abundance in every area of your life. Most of all, you will connect into the ultimate union with your own DNA cellular Oneness—a state that exists beyond the suffering and pain of living in separation from your True Self.

You will discover that *BE*:

- Awakens, clears, and aligns the body, mind, and soul for the healing, expansion, and empowerment of each individual.
- Ignites and initiates the heart, soul, and Spirit into ONEness through progressive steps that support the self-realization of truth and love as the blueprint to live one's unique personal and universal mission.
- Unwinds and clears the old threads of suffering and illusion to reveal a new matrix of being, living, and integrating the facets of one's divine and human Self into direct relationship with Infinite Source.
- Serves to evolve and heal our global community. Through teaching how to live in the light of one's Whole Self, we can begin to heal the cultural, racial, religious, spiritual, interpersonal, political, business, creative, sexual, educational, and leadership splits and challenges that confine and repress us.

You might wonder how can *BE* accomplish all of this? How can you simultaneously accomplish living your everyday life and fulfilling your daily responsibilities while integrating your body-mind-heart and soul, finding and living your mission, and BEing true to your Self? Sounds like a pretty tall order, doesn't it?

Here in *BE: The Humanity Blueprint* you will find the tools to help you clear your past, be in the now, step on to your higher destiny path in career, work, love, relationships, and with money. It can be done. I have done it, and I have guided many people through these awakenings and activations. Your unique blueprint revealed through this work provides the clarity you need to take the steps through each facet of your Self. Your goal may be to become the best person you can be, discover your life purpose, find and sustain a loving partnership, evolve yourself spiritually, heal yourself and others, develop and grow your business, visionary or entrepreneurial skills, recreate your life, end an addiction, become enlightened, awaken yourself to uplift the world, successfully implement your vision for humanity, or to *just BE*. Whatever your goal or purpose, the information and guidance that you will receive in *BE* will put you on your track, not anyone else's, to experience how to create, discover, and put into action the jewels of your soul and soar.

Where You Stand

For centuries, your spiritual abilities and courage to pursue true spiritual wisdom and create your life from your relationship with your True Self have been slowly or sometimes abruptly destroyed or negated. We have lived in a collective culture of denying the fact that we are able, and given the right, to have a direct connection to the light and power of Infinite Source. The part of your mind that evolved to block you and keep you from

INTRODUCTION

being your True Self is your ego. Its job has been to keep the door locked to the real you and to help you deal with situations that you did not know how to deal with as a young child.

At first, having an ego to protect the innocence of our young inner child self feels safe, but then when it begins to block and shut down our True Self, our talents, and ambitions from a heart and soul level, the ego begins to tear a person down. In the old paradigm, the more of an ego a person develops, the more he/she is respected. This model has not worked and has created the suffering and pain that humanity is now playing out on all levels. The new paradigm teaches how to stop giving our power over to the ego and to discover and release the radiance and divine intelligence of our True Self into our life endeavors.

Without knowing it, you have lost your ability to walk through the fires of your own soul and Spirit because fear has and still is the way that humanity is being controlled and taught how to exist. In *BE,* you will be guided on how to restore your ability to BE ONE with your Whole Self and learn to live from a new, interconnected center of love and power that will free you from fear and give you the tools to hold your own power, truth, and light. Your lost abilities will be reignited and aligned in your consciousness to help you step through the social, familial, ancestral, and karmic patterns that have blocked you and have created your self-doubt, self-rejection, and disconnection to your truth. Instead, you will experience being guided to walk your life path into the expanding, evolving, and enlightening YOU.

Your mind—when liberated of its ego, fears, and stories—has the humble opportunity to serve the highest desires of your soul's expressions. When the energy bodies that surround your soul are cleared, healed, and liberated, you are able to access and live your higher aspirations, heal your self, and live in love.

Your physical body, when aligned to your soul, has the function to receive and transmute your spiritual and emotional energies into positive, life-giving energies. When they are integrated, you are able to move through every situation in your life with grace, strength, clarity, health, and integrity. When you live in the center of your heart, your world changes. The desires that you have shift from identifying with who you want to be into BEing who you really are and realizing that you are here to serve. You find the courageous and unlimited YOU, and feel yourself growing out of old skins, old attachments, and old fears. Your body and mind feel free to live beyond the limitations that you once believed were who you are. You move from identifying yourself with your false Self and the trappings of your ego, into a more connected and whole person. You learn how to see with open eyes from an open heart.

Your life is an opportunity to be the expression of the light and power of your soul. When you are physically and spiritually integrated, what you need and desire for your highest evolution and growth come to you. As you become aligned as the WHOLE YOU, the purpose of your soul and the universe join hands. You can accomplish shedding your layers, releasing the fears in your heart, and fully opening the portal to the Infinite Source within you.

Your life is a spiritual adventure, and the more you access the powers of your soul and Spirit in your everyday life, the greater you can love, live, and succeed at what ultimately is most important in life—feeling and BEing ONE with the Source of life, the Infinite Source of your BEing, the Source of your happiness and fulfillment.

You are about to embark upon a journey that reveals the Source Codes of your soul, which, once ignited and activated, have the power to open the gateways of your mind, heart, and soul and allow you to BE what you came into this lifetime to BE. You will be touched and guided into the truths within you that will literally set you free, just as thousands of individuals over the last four decades have done through this work.

INTRODUCTION

Whether you are first starting out or have actively pursued your personal awakening for decades, you will find life changing tools to unlock the inner and outer doors to BEing connected to your most real and authentic Self. You will emanate who you are from your core because you will step into BEing ONE and whole.

What Can You Expect & What's In It For You?

BE: The Humanity Blueprint will assist you to awaken, realize, and complete the patterns and lessons that have prevented you from stepping fully into living your life purpose and to BE the light that you are. *BE: The Humanity Blueprint* teaches the skills to bring you into direct connection with Infinite Source and to live and create your life from your Whole Self. We are going to take the steps into the center of your Self where your body, mind, Spirit, and soul meet. From this access point, you will be able to experience and implement the multi-dimensional knowledge, wisdom, and consciousness that is within you.

You will receive a new level of freedom that is beyond how you have been living up until now. You will be given a medicine bag of tools that will help you discover and live your life from your Original Self, and discover first-hand how to step through the "looking glass of your life." You will be guided into living in direct connection with your truth, spiritual gifts, and life force energies to manifest your Original Self into all facets of your life—increasing relationship intimacy and stability, integrating financial abundance, and living your life purpose, career, and Bodymind wholeness.

You will be given the inside information that will awaken and show you how to access the new codes of Infinite Source that are within you to be able to move through fear, self-doubt, familial, ancestral, past life, and present life karmas. You will be guided through the trappings and unhappiness of living through ego consciousness and find true inner peace and courage. You will learn how to awaken and be guided by your True Self and fulfill your highest destiny path.

As the light, love, and power of your True Self integrate in your Bodymind and soul, it makes possible fulfilling your personal spiritual and worldly aspirations. Our destination is to unwind the sanskaras—the impressions and beliefs that you have created over lifetimes and to clear them. You will be able to walk through the door into the illuminated realms of light that reveal your True Self and provide you with direct connection to infinite love, intelligence, and power. All of the tools needed to take the next steps of your path of awakening and BEingness are here in the four volumes of *BE: The Humanity Blueprint* and in the training Intensives, which you can find out more about at www.ianalahi.com.

BE will teach you how to leave behind living in fear and compartmentalized thinking; physical, emotional, and spiritual separation; and the ways that you reject being in the infinite love and power within yourself. You will clear and liberate yourself so you access the soul language within your Whole Self and BE fully expressed.

BE teaches you how to heal your personal wounds from the roller coaster ride of your life circumstances with the intention to awaken and liberate your soul light and power. From the integrated perspective of your divine feminine and masculine selves meeting in union, the roadmap reveals how to live fully awakened and to embody your highest vibrational levels of consciousness. You will be able to move forward and upward into individual awakening and find your purpose on the collective level to serve and elevate others.

BE will guide you to live from your soul; integrate your heart and your mind; live in abundant creative energies; know real

INTRODUCTION

love; feel confident to live in your spiritual power and know how to use it wisely; live in the union of your human and divine will; unify your divine masculine and feminine energies; stand in the center of your truth; discriminate wisely; live from a 360-degree perspective, develop the ability to see, hear, and feel the guidance of your Whole Self; create relationships based upon self-awareness; experience and live with honesty, devotion, and joy; leave behind living in the separation and isolation of the soul that perpetuates ignorance, limitation, and fear; and return to the freedom that is your birthright.

You become the love and power that guides, supports, inspires, ignites, and births what you came here to do from a place of balance, integrity, and integration. You experience a new way of being in relationship to yourself by being able to see, feel, and know the infinite intelligence of your integrated Self. You will feel fearless surrender to your true path. How you make money, make love, create joy, and succeed in your endeavors, relationships, and projects will align.

When you are activating, initiating, and integrating every aspect of your human and divine Self into Oneness, you naturally become empowered. You do not have to try to BE. You become the energies that are abundantly within you that gift your life with prosperity on all levels. *BE* will guide you through your most challenging obstacles by integrating your soul into Spirit, aligning your energy bodies in light, opening your heart, healing your mind and body, initiating your spiritual power, and becoming ONE with Infinite Source. You may feel connected to Infinite Source like you have never been before and feel, hear, and know what is best for you in each situation to walk or fly with clarity and trust.

Each of us are made of divine feminine and masculine energies, which, when reconnected, align us into Oneness with Infinite Source. By integrating our divine masculine and feminine energies in our body, mind, and soul, we can heal the inner split that is underlying all political, economic, cultural, and religious untruths.

The purpose of the BE work is to give you the tools to experience divine union by transforming and lifting all of you up into BEING a conscious co-creator with Infinite Source.

While walking through the gateways to BE and practicing the meditations and exercises given, you will learn how to do the following:

LIGHT & DARK

- Activate light energy in your body.
- Experience light as the healer, integrator, initiator, activator, enlightener, and wayshower.
- Feel the light as medicine for your physical, mental, emotional, and soul bodies.
- Accept the parts of yourself that have lived in darkness out of neglect.
- Open your consciousness in all of your *Power Point Centers*.
- Ignite the channel of light within your body, your *Power Point Centers*, and your soul to align your consciousness into Oneness.
- Be directly connected to Infinite Source.
- Heal your sexuality as you allow the clear light of Source to move and live in all of your *Power Point Centers*.
- Integrate the love from your highest ray of light in your soul into each power *Power Point Center*.

INTRODUCTION

BODYMIND & SOUL

- Surrender into your soul and become the love within you.
- Release your ancestral and karmic patterns that block the light and power of your soul.
- See, feel, and BE with the creative power and divine brilliance existing beneath the anger, hurt, grief, sadness, etc. of an aspect of your soul.
- BE ONE with all aspects of your soul that behold tremendous love and power.
- Discover the source of Infinite Intelligence by going beyond the limitations of living in your mind alone.
- Develop a new mind-body connection that embraces the consciousness of your entire body.
- Come out of numbness, denial, and pain by discovering the life revealed within the union of your Bodymind and soul.
- Recognize when your mind wants to control, defend, or protect itself by shutting out the light of love because of fear.
- Fearlessly seek out the next level of your soul ready for expression, and find your footing amidst uncertainty and the unknown.
- Recognize your ego and instead of avoiding it, transform your relationship to it. Love it and direct its evolution until it has nowhere else to go except back to Source.
- Release your belief systems of how things should be. Go beyond fear.
- Reconnect the parts of your soul that hold the keys to your spiritual power and step into your life from integration and wholeness.

DIVINE ENERGIES & SELF

- Experience the functions of your divine masculine and feminine energies in your daily life.
- Integrate your masculine and feminine energies through divine acceptance.
- Experience the light of your divine masculine and feminine energies merging into One light and transforming your Bodymind and soul into Spirit.
- Awaken and realign the aspects of your Self that have been wounded and denied their existence with the light.
- Learn to let go of how you mentally and energetically hold back from the authentic expression of your True Self.
- Feel connected to your authentic voice.
- Experience the union of love and power in your Bodymind and soul.
- Reunite your higher Self, light body, physical, mental, emotional, etheric and soul bodies to awaken into love.
- Create your ideal life based upon knowing and trusting who you are.
- Know yourself. BE One with the light that you are. Find your illuminated Self.

BEING

- Hold many levels of awareness at the same time.
- Experience your spiritual, and intuitive gifts develop as a by-product of being aligned to Source.
- Learn to flow through your body and release the tensions and separations by moving and living in and with Infinite Source.

INTRODUCTION

- Acknowledge the presence of your inner spiritual teachers. Give gratitude for what you are being given.
- Fearlessly let go of needing to feel "safe" and be able to walk off the cliff into unknown possibility and feel loved and protected by your Light Team, Spiritual Masters, and Angels.
- Discover how to BE the union of your human and divine selves in every area of your life.
- Ignite, receive, and embrace the love within yourself.
- Learn to live through yourself instead of another and walk through the gateway into the ultimate relationship with yourself and others.
- Become ONE in Spirit and command your life forward by BEing ONE with Infinite Source and love.
- Experience living mastery.
- Know who you are and LOVE yourself.
- Live in joy and fulfillment.
- Become the truth ignitor, peacemaker, healer, leader, or creative BEing that expresses your Divine Self.

As you discover your unique relationship and expression with Infinite Source, allow the richness of your Spirit and soul to surrender to the light within you and from here create a life of abundant happiness, peace, and prosperity.

May all challenges and sorrows that come into your life be received and seen as gifts to help you grow and push you on to your highest rung of service and self expression. Trust the voice of truth within you as you step out of the old paradigm of fear and control into the new paradigm of infinite love as the new power in our world.

The New Source Codes For Humanity

Everyone wants to love and be loved, but first you must BE love. When you open into the Primary Source Code of existence, you recognize that you are love. In order for that love to be fully expressed and evolve the DNA structure of who you are, it has to be aligned and integrated into the light of your Whole Self. This is the secret to healing and BEing.

Imagine being aware of a Source Code that has always been within you, but only now is awakening. Imagine being able to awaken to who you really are as a human being and fully implement it into your life. Imagine a feeling of deep inspiration and trust to pursue your destiny and persevere through your life challenges and hardships with greater strength and sourced intuition. Imagine feeling less pulled down by the things that cannot be controlled and changed, but empowered to take action to bring forth your highest vision, greatest dreams, and goals of your Whole Self. Imagine living in the union of love and power while bridging and mending the separations and splits within you. This is the new foundation of wholeness and Oneness to help you BE all that you came here to BE.

The Codes of Humanity

Within the DNA of our consciousness live the imprints from all states of evolution. The lower and higher natures of our BEing are all contained within us—from our beginning as earth matter to our progression into animal and eventual human form. Subconsciously programmed into the human psyche are the animal instincts of survival intertwined with the drive to transmute lower energies into awakened awareness and to become One with God. The human condition is a story of the struggles and conflicts between the most base and most enlightened aspects of us. We wrestle with our human drives, desires, and frailties and our divine inner light and dark—all which expand and contract us as soul beings.

The continuum of our evolution has been a journey through the separation and reconnection of the human soul and God—Infinite Source—over eons of time. Most of us in recent times have existed as the walking wounded, either searching for the answer or closing off to the call within our souls to BE ONE. Yet we, humanity, are inexplicably moving toward the divine light and ONENESS consciousness that dwells within each of us.

We have come full circle exploring our lower natures, even though it has not yet manifested in the structures and systems of our lives. The sorrow, pain, pride, delusions, greed, fear, control, and arrogance that we each must face and release to become free and whole are the by-products of our evolutionary soul process. The release of these traits developed through thousands of years from the misuse of power and love is crucial to our movement forward on a universal level.

We are in a pivotal point in history where the dark and the light are in extreme conflict. The old structures created from being unconscious and separate from Infinite Source can no longer serve the direction of our destined planetary evolution.

The present transitional time period is meant to help us release the beliefs and behaviors that bind and separate us on the inside and keep us from one another and God. Union with the divine nature of our humanness is the next wave of our evolution. But, first we must learn how to face the darkness within ourselves to find the light waiting there for us to embrace.

A new paradigm is presently being birthed and will continue to flourish as we move towards a monumental shift point between 2025–2035. Knowing how to BE in the light to shift out of negative thinking; confront adversity, judgment, and fear; and unify our body, mind, and soul with divine intelligence is a necessity in order to move forward both individually and globally in this time. As we shift into a new era of integrating our physical, soul, etheric, and energetic bodies into unified alignment, we can universally cross the bridge into conscious BEING.

Coded within the cells and DNA of your body is the remembrance of BEing One with Infinite Source. You are a spiritual being of light expressed in human form that carries the Primary Source Code of the universe within your body. Collectively, we have separated and lost touch with this essence of who we are. However, the DNA coding within us is presently being activated, with or without our conscious recognition of what is occurring.

The Wisdom of Divine Intelligence

For thousands of years, we have received messages, instructions, and soul initiations to awaken us to who we really are. We have been given Source Codes to awaken the evolutionary blueprint that lies within each one of us. The great Master Beings that came to expand and enlighten humanity and to awaken our direct experience with the light and Infinite Source as we evolved through the spiritual and physical realities of life on planet Earth were all divine expressions of the One Source God.

At this time in herstory, we are being given the Source Codes to successfully come out of living in separation and fear through experiencing direct connection to our True Self.

While the Source Codes of every age have created religions and spiritual paths for people to follow, many of the most powerful and advanced spiritual beings bringing this information and instruction have not created a religion or formal spiritual path. Instead, they've come to reveal the reality of our true selves and offer insights, tools, and techniques to tap the inherent BEingness of God in each and every person. They focus on the seemingly simple, yet challenging task to release our illusions and attachments to the Self as we know it and to realize our True Self. They ask us to open, clear, align, and integrate our energetic bodies and consciousness into Oneness and guide the total surrender of the ego, so we can experience God as our True Self.

The Source Codes do not need an external religious form, belief system, or ceremonial practice to be received and implemented. They can simply be received and felt through a person's body, heart center, and soul. The codes may be experienced through a spiritual practice, but also through music, movement, dance, writing, art, the voice, pure love, or direct experiences felt within our energetic bodies through BEing One with Infinite Source, where we see, feel, and hear through the heart of the soul. The brain and soul can be activated and integrated by opening to internal frequencies of light, music, color, and love through the heart center to awaken connection with the divine. Silence and inner listening awakens the "nothing and the everything" that is received through patience, devotion, and surrender. These blissful moments give people the direct experience of BEing One in their daily lives.

The New Sources Codes for Humanity are a synthesis of spiritual wisdom and instruction on how to spiritually integrate and move into ONENESS. They are energetic, spiritual, etheric, and soul codes that transform our hearts, soul, psyche, body, and Spirit. They are not a new religion but a direct, experiential pathway that harnesses all that is inherent in our divine and human natures. They can be felt in the body as energy, love and light, and in the mind as enlightening awareness, experienced as Oneness consciousness.

They are the kernels of wisdom and living awareness that heal the pain and victimhood that humanity continues to experience and many are presently working to overcome. They are the gateways to living in a new, integrated consciousness where body, mind, Spirit, and soul are ONE. The Source Codes are experienced as presence, direct knowledge, wisdom, power, and bliss. They are frequencies encoded in love direct from Infinite Source and absent of the fear and control that often govern physical reality.

Ending the Illusion of Separation

Our human source coding is very simple. We are all expressions of God in physical form. We have always been connected with God—Infinite Source because *we are of Source.* That is our Primary Source Code. It is the foundation that enables us to transform from darkness to light. Yet as a collective, we have established standards and created illusions that have altered our ability to realize that there is no separation.

The powers that presently govern our world are split between protecting the good of the many and the interests of a limited few. An old paradigm of illusion and imbalanced power continues to rule. It involves keeping the masses asleep, choosing hatred over love, manipulating policies and laws to fulfill one's own grandiosities, creating and maintaining fear, and leading others from being aligned with the darkness of control and manipulation. As a world culture, we have been taught how to shut down our minds, immune systems, hearts, and souls by living in fear and in violation of our own spiritual power. As a result, we experience separation, hidden and obvious despair, dullness, numbness, avoidance, and lack.

Living in separation from Infinite Source has split us apart inside and has created internal battlefields. We have compartmentalized our body-mind-soul into hidden vaults within our selves and have created an inner battle between our subconscious and unconscious selves, between our light and dark. These separations are the underlying reason for our own internal abandonment, rejection, self-sabotage, and betrayal and the root of external hatred, fear, arrogance, and greed. They prevent us from stepping into our highest light and creating social standards for the highest good of humanity.

Given our internal separation, we often feel like we are an island unto ourselves. We fail to see the expansive consequences of our intentions, words, and deeds on humanity. Yet, our individual evolution is deeply tied into the evolution of the planet. Most of the social, political, financial, environmental, and religious outrages occurring on the planet in this present moment are battles between the light of awakening and illumination, and the dark of deadened awareness, control, manipulation, and denial. As we each choose to become responsible for how we love and use our power with others and in the world, we will stop the dishonoring and destruction of mother earth and her inhabitants.

The New Source Codes help humanity end the internal inner battles of hatred, shame, blame, and fear and shift into a new integrated dynamic of love and power. Our human evolution can no longer be accomplished through the battles between our subconscious and unconscious selves. The Source Codes contain the transformative power of light that strengthen and elevate the subconscious and unconscious selves into Oneness and helps us to awaken and trust our True Self instead of giving our power over to a False Self. When the Source Codes are physically embodied, the False Self can no longer exist.

The New Source Codes of Humanity that are given in all four volumes of *BE: The Humanity Blueprint* support you to discover how you naturally express your divine Oneness with Infinite Source. They awaken and empower the sleeping genes of higher love and power within you. They help you see, feel, and embody the truth, reality, and meaning of your existence by overhauling the old ways that you have created to compartmentalize your life. They restructure your *thinking-feeling-being* nature into a new matrix of inter-connectedness. Once ignited in the body, they activate your whole brain DNA light grid.

Embodying the Source Codes turns on the switch to living and BEing in a 360-degree perspective. The codes naturally prompt the opening of your higher survival instincts rather than your lower ones. When your consciousness is blazing in the light of love, the parts of you that exist in a disconnected state from Infinite Source can and will heal themselves through the process of integration. Your mind shifts from being a lone and fearful wolf to being concerned about the pack. You shift from being self-centered and living in fear and denial to BEing centered in Self and living in love. Everyday living that involves our partner, our family, our co-workers, our neighbors, our community, and the world at large are seen through a new lens. We begin to give ourselves permission to leave behind the beliefs that we have used to create separation within ourselves and with others.

Presently, the spiritual realms are asking us to open and let go of the ways that we habitually control circumstances and our own life force energies. We are being asked to suspend and release judgment and fear, and allow for the impossible to become possible. Such is the power of divine intelligence, which provides us with the opportunity to choose between truth and illusion.

How the Source Codes Express in Your Life

The Source Codes presented in *BE* are the steps to activate your own personal evolutionary blueprint and empowerment. You will experience the Source Codes as you walk the path of soul integration and embrace the parts of yourself that have been ignored, abandoned, and forgotten. You will harness the currents of love existing in the cells of your body to open, transmute, transform, and align into the highest light of Infinite Source within you. You will experience the Source Codes when you discover and unite the depth and beauty of your divine masculine and feminine energies as the gateway to infinite love, power, and light. You will experience the codes when you transform the relationship between your mind-psyche-ego and heart center. You will experience a DNA shift into light when your present perception of your identity shifts from the mental plane into the soul and higher dimensional planes of light.

To say *YES* to the Source Codes within you requires a willingness to suspend disbelief and trust the guidance and love of the universe cloaked in your higher Self, waiting to be received. Sometimes a move to a new place, changing one's diet, reinventing your job description with life, starting a new business, taking a much needed risk, saying how you feel, having a baby, leaving behind the life that you knew, traveling, getting married, changing careers, or healing an illness can activate your personal and Imprint Source Code.

Imprint Source Codes

Within each of us dwells one Imprint Source Code, or a series of Imprint Source Codes, that serve as the foundation to BE and live fully as your True Self. Imagine a state of BEing that is as flowing as a waterfall, solid as a mountain, spacious as the sky, and deep as the ocean. Your Imprint Source Code is a spark of Oneness consciousness that is found by opening and integrating your heart, spiritual power, soul essence, and divine intelligence. It holds the secret mission of who you are and takes you into alignment with infinite love in all of its forms and expressions. Your Imprint Source Code is discovered through a process of expansion beyond normal everyday thinking. It can be used to find and implement your life path of service and joy.

We each have a specific function as a unique and distinctive code of light. The love that you are dwells inside of your Imprint Source Code essence. When awakened and aligned to, all of the right circumstances, people, and opportunities come to support you as you step into creating your life from your Imprint Source Code.

As an Imprint Source Code carrier, you have the ability to explore, create, and complete your destiny. If you become aware to which codes you are aligned it will help you to accept and step into your authentic mission.

The Imprint Source Codes manifest as the following 22 expressions of Infinite Source. Each code provides a life lesson to learn. You may be a single Imprint Source Code or a mix of a few different types of codes. The more you have, the more there is to understand and master in a lifetime.

Imprint Source Codes

Imprint Source Code	Purpose and Expression	Life Lessons
Awakeners	One who brings the abilities of living love with the Absolute and envelopes others with their realization	Listening to your intuition, allowing for differences, and letting go of carrying universal and personal pain
Birthers	Open the gateways for the continuation of creation to occur	Creating long-term friendships, releasing fear, following one's own dreams, not giving away one's power
Bridges	Create understanding, acceptance, and new insights between two or more contrasting and different realities and perceptions	Appreciation for differences, seeing outside the box, opening the heart, releasing fixed opinions
Creators	Bring newly manifested energies into form	Practicing self-acceptance, self-love, surrender, and receptivity
Experiencers	Approach all of life with wonder, offering humanity the opportunities to release and let go of the past	Seeing the big and small picture at the same time, taking responsibility, thinking about others and their well-being, honesty, commitment
Gods and Goddesses	Encompass the strengths, powers, love, and harmony of all facets of heaven and earth	Sexual balance, truthfulness, soul reconnection, integrating light and dark, letting go of control

Imprint Source Code	Purpose and Expression	Life Lessons
Healers	Clear, reconnect, and align the physical and spiritual energies that restore Oneness with the Original Self and Infinite Source	Holding boundaries, practicing detachment, releasing the ego, integration, self-care, selflessness, surrender
Igniters	Energetic initiators of the heart and soul	Learning grounding, letting go of outcomes and all judgment
Integrators	Reestablish the balance, healing, and harmony between people, societies, nations, and the world	Being creative, honoring one's family, living a health-based lifestyle
Interpreters	Awaken the soul through writing, music, art, movement, film making, singing, etc.	Balance, avoiding extremes, trust, letting go, fearlessness
Justice and Truth Initiators	Shine the positive virtues of responsibility, moving through darkness, and instilling the desire to live in peace	Integrating the heart center, emotions, practicing forgiveness and gratitude, keeping energy shields strong, not taking on other's imbalances
Leaders	Initiate the power in others and themselves to enlighten their abilities to be in duality and be free of duality	Allowing others to expand, supporting the power and voice of others
Liberators	Free the mind and soul to pursue truth and establish freedom	Self-love, self-care, intimacy, protection of one's inner heart, creative strength

Imprint Source Code	Purpose and Expression	Life Lessons
Lovers	Awaken others to love just by being who they are	Non-projection, moving through denial and addiction, practicing self-responsibility
Messengers	Servants of Spirit who master their connection with Infinite Source to deliver information that uplifts, transforms, and evolves others	Keeping things simple, practicing detachment, allowing others to be exactly who and what they are, and forgiveness
Nurturers	Connect life energy, sustain love, and are reminders of Mother-Father God in every moment and action	Practicing non-reactivity, expressing their own creative voice, taking time to be alone, doing nothing, practicing silence, detachment
Peace Makers	Initiate the awakening of universal awareness beyond duality; serve to end living in internal fragmentation, and separation and pain as a gateway to compassion, understanding, and love	Healing the splits within oneself, ending self-hatred, understanding the power of choice, healing the heart, stepping into fearless truth on all levels
Preservers	Heal and maintain the internal structures of a society, the oceans, the earth, and all life forms	Gratitude and acceptance for what is
Researchers	Discover solutions to problems that plague humanity	Releasing the ego, remembering mind-body integration, BEing heart-centered.

Imprint Source Code	Purpose and Expression	Life Lessons
Seers	Bridge multi-dimensions of consciousness for the purpose of guiding others to reach the light.	Creating boundaries, enjoying life, receiving joy from the connection with Spirit, trusting others and One Self.
Teachers	Instill the love of learning, expanding oneself, and creating a foundation for advancing one's Self.	Creating joy and curiosity and avoiding rigidity and fixed opinions
Visionaries	Bring into form the expansions of awareness needed to catapult humanity forward globally	Accomplishing short and long term tasks, remaining grounded, healing one's own pain, self-judgment, and suffering, releasing DNA blocks, living in love

Spirit Gateways®/Iana Lahi All Rights Reserved ©

As you discover and implement the lessons and gifts of your Imprint Source Code, you will feel confident enough to embody what you stand for. You will find yourself wanting to feed your body vibrant thoughts and food; give your emotional body compassion, acceptance, and forgiveness; and provide your mind non-judgment and non-duality thinking. You will find yourself surrendering to your own truth. You will become uninterested in finding fault or blame for yourself or others. You will become a generator of life force energies and a portal into infinite love. You will feel connected to your life with new anticipation, faith, and commitment because you have left behind the box that you created for yourself and all of the false illusions that went with the packaging of your beliefs.

BE: THE HUMANITY BLUEPRINT INTRODUCTION

When the voice of ego and mind counter-attack your real Self, you will know how to BE in the center of your heart and release what feels worn out, counter productive, and unsupportive to the enlightening you.

The Source Code themes found within the BE work reestablish and permanently link your heart-mind-soul to BE ONE. Your Whole Self is birthed into the matrix of light and has the ability to heal, empower, and transform you. Within each of the *BE* volumes, the information to discover and open the Source Codes within you are there for the taking. You just have to choose to experience and live them. They are the keys to your inner kingdom.

The Source Codes for these times are given, activated, and guided through *BE: The Humanity Blueprint.*

Through following the Codes outlined in *BE*, you will:

- Create healing by clearing your genetic and karmic DNA structures.
- Ignite and align the *Power Point Centers*.
- Awaken and enlighten your soul.
- Reconnect the lost powers and love within the soul.
- Unite your heart and mind.
- Melt the resistances in the mind and body.
- Transform your relationship to ego.
- Release limiting ancestral patterns.
- Open to multi-dimensional realities.
- Reunite, purify, transform, and integrate your divine masculine and feminine energies.
- Heal your sexuality.
- Awaken the right use of power.
- Learn how to love yourself and others unconditionally.
- Know how to honor children for their divine intelligence.

- Open the gateways to live in Infinite Love.
- Unite the codes of love and power as a personal and global pathway to truth and freedom.
- Implement light as a healing force both personally and into the structures of society and the planet.

This Can Be Done

It is said that a hallmark of effective teaching involves not just imparting knowledge or information to an audience, but also providing a practical demonstration of the subject matter to validate its real life relevance and possibility. In other words, people need to know that following this stuff actually works, and more importantly, can work for them. As a messenger and bringer of the Source Codes, I have made a commitment to BE impeccable with how I deliver this work. I have personally practiced and lived everything that I share. I have experienced Infinite Source working through me with ferocious focus and clarity, as I have shared this work with others to go beyond what they thought would be possible, yet always yearned for. It can be done. Anyone can do this. However, I must remind you that this work is not just about being read or understood conceptually. It must be felt, experienced, and lived. It is not a spiritual practice to "take up" as something separate from your everyday life. It becomes a moment-to-moment choice to go beyond your comfort zones, BE ONE with Infinite Source, and experience it as close as your heartbeat. The gift of being a human being is having the opportunity to discover that Infinite Source—God—lives through you *as YOU*.

I am here for each and every one of you to help you discover your own blueprint and codes, whether we meet in person or not. My intentions are to help ignite and support as many of you as I can, whether man or woman, young or old, and regardless of religion, nationality, creed, or spiritual beliefs. My heart is One with yours, and I pray that I can serve in the highest way to support your awakening, upliftment, and realization to BE One. BE You.™

May the source of light become your inspiration and joy.

May love fill you, surround you, and heal you.

May your heart BE happy.

May you always know that you are never alone.

May you trust that your prayers are being heard.

May you embrace your life lessons as gateways into aliveness, truth, and grace.

May you remember who you are.

May you realize that you are eternal.

And blessed in love.

To Conclude

BE Priorities

"To BE or not to BE, that is the question..."

You are beginning a journey to reconnect with the eternal blueprint of who you are—your Original Self. It is a journey inward, outward, and forward that will ultimately lead you to the true home within you and your connection to all that is. It goes beyond all techniques, yet encompasses the essence of all practices.

Before the sun rises, before you get out of bed, before you begin the rush to "do" your life, consider these **BE Priorities** to help you **BE in life.** They are your guideposts on your journey. If you ever feel lost or unsure about where you are going, remember this "spiritual unpacking" list for your trip.

These **BE Priorities** are the practices that you can bring into your daily life. They will link who you truly are into every aspect of your life. They are the positive expressions that naturally emanate from your connections to your soul and the Infinite Source of all life.

BE: THE HUMANITY BLUEPRINT INTRODUCTION

BE Priorities

1. **BE willing to suspend disbelief.**	Take a moment to let go of needing to believe only what you can physically see.
2. **BE responsible for how you feel.**	How you respond to the ways you need others to see, hear, and feel you are your responsibility. Develop your ability to respond to your own needs and desires with love.
3. **BE open and flexible.**	Pay attention to how you shut yourself down and what supports you to be open and curious.
4. **BE willing to let go of being right and in control.**	Take a risk and choose to be happy over needing to be right.
5. **BE honest with yourself.**	Develop your internal witness, which can truthfully access your desires, thoughts, and actions.
6. **BE a better listener.**	Count to 10 before you speak while in conversation with someone else. Listen from your heart. Take in the energy behind the words.
7. **BE willing.**	Put aside your standard responses and habits. Feel the desire to do things differently. Try new ways of thinking and behaving.

BE PRIORITIES

8. BE accepting.	When relating with others, receive them exactly how they are without trying to change them, or impose your immediate need onto them. What a person shares with you may be exactly what they need to express in order to have a breakthrough.
9. BE with yourself.	Stay present with yourself. Live in the moment in full presence. Bring your focus into solar plexus, and you will know what you feel.
10. BE courageous.	Go beyond your comfort zone. Pray for courage if nothing else to reach beyond your limits.
11. BE authentic.	Let go of trying to be like anyone else. Treasure who you are. Live as YOU fully.
12. BE kind.	Love your enemy. Create loving kindness with all and you will help others grow into being whole.
13. BE centered in your heart.	There is nowhere to go except into your heart. When you are centered in it, there is no room to run. See life from the center of the universe, and be prepared for life to pour its abundance into you.

BE: THE HUMANITY BLUEPRINT INTRODUCTION

14. BE willing to let go of your identity.	Who you "really are" is not who you think yourself to be. Who you are is beyond all roles and identifications. Go into the big emptiness of not knowing. Trust that who you are will be revealed as you let go of trying to be anything.
15. BE conscious.	Stay awake. Listen, see, and feel from your connection in the light within your body, heart, and soul.
16. BE connected.	Come out of separation. Hug a tree. Hold yourself. Connect into the truth within you. Acknowledge the love within you.
17. BE respectful of your body.	Treat your body with care, love, and respect, and develop the wisdom to know it as a sacred temple and chalice of the divine.
18. BE the driver of your destiny.	Stay behind the wheel. End sitting in the back seat of your life. Stop giving away your power to others. Take risks to be who you are and to say what is real for you.
19. BE love.	This is the most important action and priority that you can ever practice. Be in the love. Embrace the love that is present everywhere and most importantly within YOU.

BE PRIORITIES

20. BE awake.	To sleepwalk through life is to waste the precious life that you have been given. To believe the fear that tries to infiltrate your life is living a lie. Stay alert to how the light wants you to be awake and enlightening.
21. BE power.	End questioning yourself. Instead, question how to find the connection with Infinite Source within you. Here, you will find authentic power.
22. BE here.	Everything that you need to learn and grow through exists in this present moment. Trust the universe. It is your ultimate teacher.
23. BE your purpose.	You have the responsibility to show up as the real you. You came into this lifetime with a specific gift and abilities to develop, which are meant to evolve your soul and the world.
24. BE the solution.	Let go of trying to fix things, reacting, blaming, judging, and defending. Choose to recognize who you are, and become the authentic you. By being whole and complete, you will trust your ideas and your input. Your actions will be the solution.

25. BE willing to fully express yourself.	Open the door to the life stream of consciousness within you, however your heart prompts you. Choose joy and explore the deeper desires to become One with sound, color, texture, emotion, passion, vibration, intellect, heart, soul, and love.
26. BE human and divine unified.	Embrace the perfection of being a human with frailties and love that need to be expressed. Embody the divine essence of Infinite Source. See through the eyes of the divine embracing your human condition. Know you are a divine being transforming your humanness in each moment.
27. BE light.	The biggest breakthroughs of your life happen when you let go of your attachments to what you hold dear, which keep you in the dark. The light has the power to heal anything. In the dark exists unmanifested raw, creative power. Allow the light to shine into what has not yet been awakened and be the awakener of light.
28. BE Whole.	As you begin your day, center your focus into your heart and feel into your mind, feelings, energy, and Spirit. Embrace them with love and open your inner space to have them merge.
29. BE YOU.	Allow the expressions and voice of your authentic Self to shine, give, lead, and BE One in every moment.

BE PRIORITIES

30. BE Happy.	Trust in your connection with the divine. Live in the moment of perfect communion with Infinite Source. Fill your heart with the radiance of light and give up worrying and doubt. Trust completely and know you are loved.
31. BE ONE.	In the Ultimate Reality there is only Oneness. All of the thoughts in your mind are illusions. BE loving to yourself and reach through all of your fears and resistances into the One Source of love. Here, you will know nothing but the eternal bliss of BEing nothing—BEing One with the Love of Infinite Source—God.

Spirit Gateways®/Iana Lahi All Rights Reserved ©

Welcome to the BE Community

For more information about

BE: The Humanity Blueprint
4-volume book series

Our signature training

The Spirit Gateways® BE System Experience

plus

Intensives, Retreats, Courses, and Facilitator Trainings

and

Spirit Gateways® Foundation

visit:

www.ianalahi.com

www.ingramcontent.com/pod-product-compliance
Lightning Source LLC
Chambersburg PA
CBHW050606300426
44112CB00013B/2094